W9-BYK-938

STEAM JOBS IN
Social Media

Kevin Walker

Rourke
Educational Media

rourkeeducationalmedia.com

Before Reading:

Building Academic Vocabulary and Background Knowledge

Before reading a book, it is important to tap into what your child or students already know about the topic. This will help them develop their vocabulary, increase their reading comprehension, and make connections across the curriculum.

1. *Look at the cover of the book. What will this book be about?*
2. *What do you already know about the topic?*
3. *Let's study the Table of Contents. What will you learn about in the book's chapters?*
4. *What would you like to learn about this topic? Do you think you might learn about it from this book? Why or why not?*
5. *Use a reading journal to write about your knowledge of this topic. Record what you already know about the topic and what you hope to learn about the topic.*
6. *Read the book.*
7. *In your reading journal, record what you learned about the topic and your response to the book.*
8. *After reading the book complete the activities below.*

Content Area Vocabulary
Read the list. What do these words mean?

blog
consultants
crucial
encompass
invention
niche
occupations
personality
philosophy
revolution

After Reading:

Comprehension and Extension Activity

After reading the book, work on the following questions with your child or students in order to check their level of reading comprehension and content mastery.

1. *Describe the events and inventions that led to the rise of social media. (Summarize)*
2. *In what ways has social media changed the world? (Infer)*
3. *Who invented the Nike swoosh? (Asking Questions)*
4. *What do data analysts look for in the information they collect? (Text to Self Connection)*
5. *What role do art fields such as writing and design play in social media? (Asking Questions)*

Extension Activity

Sign up for a kid-friendly social media site with adult permission. Post text and photos, and study how the technology works. What postings prove to be the most popular? Have you made any new friends with a common interest? See where working with social media can take you!

TABLE OF CONTENTS

What is STEAM?. 4
What Is Social Media? 6
Engineer and Manager Jobs 13
Digital Media 22
Creating Content, Crunching Numbers. 26
Marketing and Public Relations. 36
Startups 40
STEAM Job Facts. 44
Glossary 46
Index 47
Show What You Know 47
Websites to Visits 47
About the Author 48

WHAT IS STEAM?

Every day, people use social media to connect with one another. Friends post pictures on Facebook. Journalists report news on Twitter. And YouTube is home to tons of funny cat videos!

YouTube, a video sharing site, was founded in California in 2005 by Chad Hurley, Steve Chen, and Jawed Karim.

Social media also creates jobs and has changed many **occupations**. These include marketing, journalism, software engineering, computer technology, and book publishing. All of this involves STEAM—science, technology, engineering, art, and math.

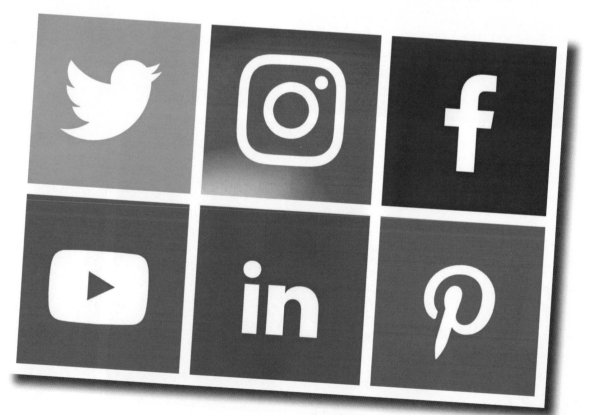

The thumbnails, or social sharing logos, of Twitter, Instagram, Facebook, YouTube, LinkedIn, and Pinterest are simple and instantly recognizable.

WHAT IS SOCIAL MEDIA?

When people think of social media, they think of Facebook and Twitter because they are so popular. However, social media can **encompass** any kind of electronic communication that allows people to share information. These include websites and applications, or apps. People use social media with their computers, tablets, and smartphones, anywhere they are in the world!

People also use social media sites to discuss topics that interest them. For example, the website Reddit allows people around the world to have conversations on everything from television shows and movies to politics and **philosophy**.

STEAM Fast Facts

Social Media Boom

The number of people use social media in the United States grew from just seven percent of the population in 2005 amazing 65 percent by

For young people, social media has always been around. However, much of it did not exist just a decade ago.

Between 2006 and 2008, new technologies, websites, products, and apps came on the market that led to social media's rise.

- **2006** Facebook opened to the public.
- **2006** Twitter launched.
- **2007** The first Apple iPhone became available.

The first iPhone was released June 29, 2007.

Facebook's color scheme is blue and white because its co-founder, Mark Zuckerberg, is red-green color blind. Blue is the color he sees best.

- **2007** Amazon released the Kindle reader.
- **2008** Google launched the Android mobile phone system.

Android was first developed as a platform for digital cameras. The founders later shifted their focus to smartphones.

Amazon Kindle's social media network allows readers to connect and share their thoughts about books.

Facebook bought Instagram in 2012 for $1 billion in cash and stock.

Social media sites continue to grow in number. They include Pinterest and Instagram, where people share photos and ideas. LinkedIn allows adults to exchange information about careers and jobs. Google+ allows people to share photos, articles, and comments, much like Facebook. There also are social media sites just for kids, such as Lego Life.

Pinterest has 150 million active monthly users.

Just think—most social media didn't even exist at the beginning of the 21st century! Social media has created a **revolution** in how people communicate. Many compare it to Johannes Gutenberg's **invention** of the printing press in the 15th century. That invention led to the spread of knowledge throughout Europe, changing the world. Social media, which connects everyone worldwide, is doing the same.

Johannes Gutenberg
(circa 1395–1468)

What Happens When You Text?

Technology works wonders every day. Here is what happens when you text someone from your phone.

- All texts use SMS (short message service).
- Texts are sent in blocks of 160 characters—that's where the "short" part comes in!
- When you tap "send," your message travels by radio waves to the nearest cell phone tower through a control channel.
- The tower sends the message through the control channel to a Short Message Service Center (SMSC).
- The SMSC receives, holds, and forwards texts. If the phone you are trying to reach is active, the text goes through. If it is not, the SMSC holds the text until the receiving phone is on.
- All this happens in seconds. It seems like magic, but it's cooler than that. It's science!

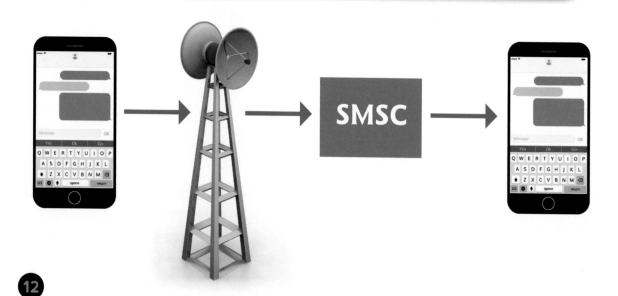

ENGINEER AND MANAGER JOBS

Real STEAM Job: *Software Engineer*

Take a look at a smartphone. All the little squares you see on the home screen are apps that connect you with whatever service you want. Software engineers design those apps, making sure they function properly.

Software engineers also design the service itself. For example, think about Facebook. Software engineers write computer code to make sure all the text, images, and videos appear properly on every page.

/www.facebook.com/   Facebook - Log in or Sign

Email or

facebook

Sign

It's free

Connect with friends and the world around you on Facebook.

First n

Mobile

New

Birthda

See photos and updates from friends in News Feed.

Month

Share what's new in your life on your Timeline.

O Fe

14 **Find more** of what you're looking for with Facebook Search.

For social media, software engineers perform a **crucial** job. They use the technology, engineering, and math portions of STEAM, especially understanding computer coding and how it works.

Facebook's software engineering interns are paid about $84,000 per year. (Source: www.glassdoor.com)

Real STEAM Job: *Social Media Manager*

People find social media so enjoyable that they use it for fun. But some people have jobs overseeing social media for companies.

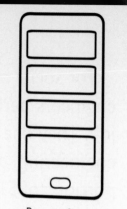

Remote Server --

Every big company—and most small ones, too—have a website about their products and social media pages on sites such as Facebook, Twitter, Pinterest, and YouTube.

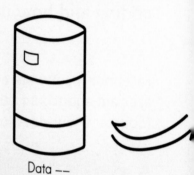

Data --

Social media managers decide what is posted on those accounts. They also communicate with customers through social media. That means they need "people skills," which is a way of saying they are good at talking to others and being good listeners. An upbeat **personality** helps, too!

Laptop -- Mini-Note --

Social ——

Mobile ——

Computer ——

Social media managers are smart about the best time and place to post something. They also know how to run a social media marketing campaign.

They draw upon several STEAM skills, especially technology and the arts!

STEAM Spotlight

Social Media at Work

These organizations put social media into action!

- European car company Dacia boosted sales by placing advertisements on Facebook.

- Red Bull energy drink reached 1.2 million people in Australia by promoting their Summer Edition drink on Instagram.

- The Girl Scouts of America got almost 20,000 people to download their app after offering it through Twitter.

Real STEAM Job: *Digital Strategy Director*

Are you interested in being the big boss? Digital strategy director is a fancy term for people who have the job of directing social media for a business. They oversee social media postings, content, and design. Sometimes they are called the Internet marketing director or digital strategist.

A digital strategist's goal is to get as many people to visit a website as possible. The ultimate prize is to become one of the most visited sites on the Web!

STEAM Fast Fact:

Most Popular Social Media

The top five most-visited social media sites based in the United States, in order of popularity, are YouTube, Facebook, Twitter, Instagram, and LinkedIn.

DIGITAL MEDIA

When your parents were growing up, they got news from two main sources: television and newspapers. Those days are long gone. Now, social media allows people to communicate information about events as they happen.

STEAM Fast Fact:

Where People Get News

About 40 percent of Americans get their news online. But among younger people, that number is 50 percent. Only 27 percent of those 18 to 29 years old get news from television and only 5 percent from newspapers.

STEAM Spotlight

Social Media Changes Communications

Here are some ways social media has changed
how we communicate:

- By 2018, an estimated 2.67 billion people will use social media.
- In the United States, people spend an average of 216 minutes per week on social media.
- About 350,000 tweets are sent around the world every minute.
- Elected leaders use social media to communicate with the people they represent.
- Doctors, nurses, and paramedics use social media platforms to quickly share patient information.

Media companies employ people who communicate news using social media, especially Twitter. They also constantly post news updates on websites. This is how many people find out what's happening in the world in the fastest way possible.

These exciting jobs require skills in technology and writing.

Journalists say publishing and promoting news stories are the most important ways they use social media. (Source: www.cision.com)

Entertainment also requires social media workers. People used to be limited to watching movies and shows at the theater or on TV. Not anymore! Now they can go to various websites to stream movies or TV shows whenever they want.

Nearly half of people surveyed worldwide say they use social media while watching shows. (Source: www.nielsen.com)

Entertainment companies need people who can work with social media to let people know the latest about the movies and shows they have available for viewing.

CREATING CONTENT, CRUNCHING NUMBERS

Real STEAM Job: *Writers and Editors*

At many companies, writers and editors develop the written content for social media posts. Some writers and editors work as **consultants**, developing and editing content for multiple companies.

Editors often research topics that will interest a company's target audience, then assign writers to write about them. Once a post is written, the editor checks it for style, accuracy, grammar, and punctuation. Writers and editors work together to create content that is interesting and written in a style that reflects the company's tone, voice, and values. A company that sells funeral services and a company that sells roller skates require different approaches to writing their content.

Writers and editors hold meetings to discuss content for social media and websites.

Start Your Own News Site!

Many people use writing and editing skills to start their own website, **blog**, or Twitter channel. Usually they focus on one **niche** topic, providing people with information on everything from politics and cooking to cars and pets.

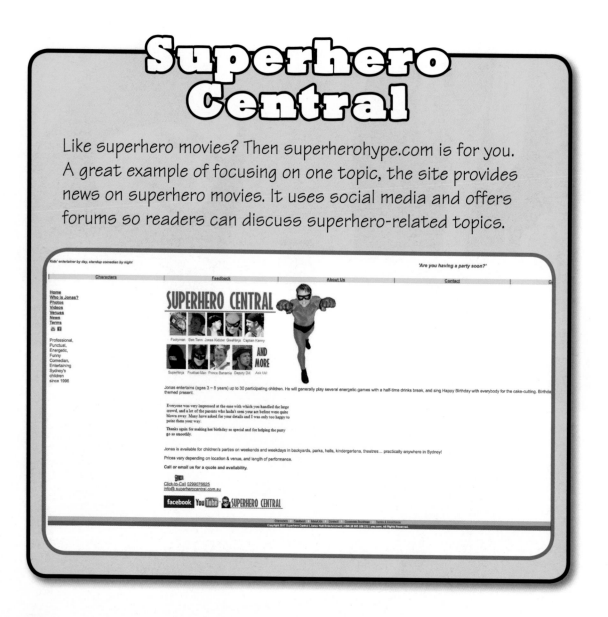

Superhero Central

Like superhero movies? Then superherohype.com is for you. A great example of focusing on one topic, the site provides news on superhero movies. It uses social media and offers forums so readers can discuss superhero-related topics.

Real STEAM Job: *Digital Designer*

People with artistic skills also have a place in social media. Digital designers create the images and the overall look of social media sites. This includes the logos and the way Web pages look whether they are viewed on your computer, tablet, or smartphone.

Digital designers must know how to apply technology to design. They use images, animation, video, and text to create attractive websites. They need to know programs such as Flash and Adobe, and understand HTML, the code used to create web pages.

Social media users like content that is interesting, attractive, and interactive. Digital designers work to develop websites and social media pages that appeal to users.

Famous Logos

Here are three famous logos and the artists who created them:

• Apple: Artist Rob Janoff came up with two designs for the Apple logo. One had a bite in it, one didn't. The late Steve Jobs, then CEO of Apple, chose the one with the bite.

Though the apple logo still has a bite, it no longer has its rainbow stripes.

• Nike: Carolyn Davidson, an art student at Portland State University, designed the famous swoosh.

• Graphic artist Milton Glaser created the "I Love N.Y." logo. His sketches of the logo are now in the Museum of Modern Art in New York City.

Real STEAM Job: *Data Analyst*

Are you good with math? Then data analysis might be the field for you. Data analysts dig deep into statistics, using large amounts of information to determine patterns and trends in social media use. This work usually involves knowing how to use computer software to gather and separate data, something that would take far too long to do by hand.

Data analysts create charts to illustrate trends in social media use.

When businesses look at data to make decisions, data analysts provide the information. This job is one of the most important for any social media site, because it helps company leaders make smart decisions. People who do this job must be good with numbers and also understand how social media data affect a business.

Social media businesses use data analysts' reports to make decisions.

Real STEAM Job: *Video Producer*

If you spend time on social media, you probably watch videos. Short videos have become the most popular aspect of social media. Companies hire video producers to make videos that promote products on social media. They must know how to work cameras, perform video editing and, most importantly, they must know what type of content is most likely to be shared. The ultimate goal: going viral!

Videos are the most consumed content on the Internet. A social media video producer develops videos based on an understanding of what people like to share.

With YouTube, you can practice this on your own. Millions of people upload videos every day. Some of them become more popular than really expensive videos made by big companies! Using the software on your home computer, you can develop the skills to make compelling videos.

Some companies create commercials and short films designed specifically for social media.

MARKETING AND PUBLIC RELATIONS

Real STEAM Job: *Marketing*

Marketers are in the business of promoting and selling products or services. People who work in marketing team up with social media managers, data analysts, writers, editors, and designers to create marketing campaigns. The purpose of a marketing campaign is to get people interested in a product.

Marketing professionals showcase the positive qualities of the companies they represent. They research potential customers and develop marketing campaigns that appeal to their needs. Social media marketers develop campaigns that are specific to the consumption and sharing habits of social media users.

Marketing managers also create contracts with advertisers, which means they need good math skills. Another key skill is creativity, which is necessary for coming up with new marketing ideas.

Marketing teams brainstorm together to develop creative ideas.

CREATIVE PROCESS

O FIX PROBLEMS

ESEARCH   Report / Case Stu...   Analysis

SION   Inspiration *** WAYS T... T NEW ID

RAINSTORM   Thinking >>

*** WAYS TO GET THE BEST

OLUTION   What / Where / W...   ...n / W

Real STEAM Job: *Public Relations*

Public relations workers promote a company and its products. They also answer questions from the media about a company. Writing is a key skill, because they have to write press releases and information on websites.

Public relations teams demonstrate products at conferences and expos.

The biggest public relations companies now have entire departments devoted to online and social media work. The job requires you to manage the company's image, or brand.

Most companies have their own pages on social media such as Facebook and Twitter.

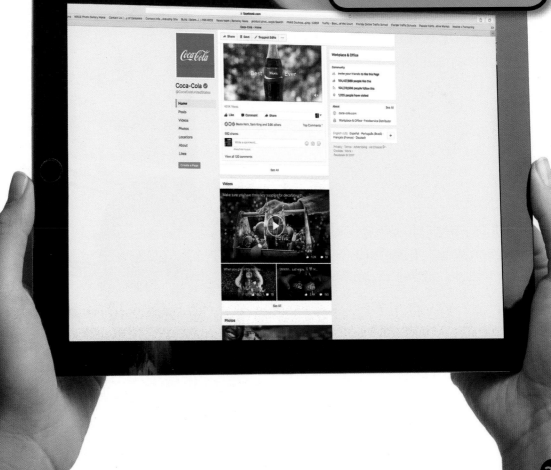

STARTUPS

In social media, invention continues at a rapid pace. Each year, new social media companies, called startups, appear that help people communicate faster around the world.

Social Media Inventors

These are some of the most famous inventors in social media:

- Mark Zuckerberg: He was the co-creator of Facebook while a student at Harvard University. It's now the most popular social media site on the planet.

- Jack Dorsey: He co-founded Twitter, which now has 313 million active monthly users.

- Kevin Systrom and Mike Krieger: They launched Instagram in 2010. The app reached 10,000 users within a few hours. Two years later, they sold the company to Facebook for $1 billion.

- Ben Silbermann: He co-founded Pinterest with architect Evan Sharp and Paul Sciarra, who used to play in a country-western band!

- Caterina Fake: Fake co-founded the image-sharing site Flickr with Stewart Butterfield after working as art director at Salon.com.

Inventing a social media app or website requires creativity, imagination, technology know-how, and a positive attitude. With more than 2 billion expected to use social media by 2018, the need for social media professionals is expected to continue growing.

STEAM Fast Fact:

Happy Accidents

Sometimes good inventions happen by accident. Caterina Fake came up with Flickr while trying to develop an online game. The game didn't work out, but the idea of sharing images did.

Will you work with an established company? Or develop your own startup? Social media is teeming with opportunities for inventors, writers, editors, marketers, and STEAM professionals alike. Which path will you take?

STEAM JOB FACTS

Software Engineers
Important skills: math, science, technology, problem-solving
Important knowledge: computer coding and systems
College major: software engineering, computer programming

Social Media Manager
Important skills: leadership, good listening skills
Important knowledge: writing, editing, customer service, communications
College majors: marketing, journalism

Digital Strategy Director
Important skills: leadership, decision-making, critical thinking
Important knowledge: technology, marketing, business
College majors: marketing, business administration

Digital Media
Important skills: writing, editing, critical thinking
Important knowledge: technology, communications
College majors: journalism, marketing, English

Digital Design

Important skills: artistic talent, problem solving, creativity

Important knowledge: digital design programs, computer coding

College majors: art, graphic design

Data Analyst

Important skills: math, technology, statistics, critical thinking

Important knowledge: computer programs, data analysis

College majors: math, computer science, economics

Video Producer

Important skills: artistic talent, decision-making, leadership, creativity

Important knowledge: video filming and editing, computer technology

College majors: film production, cinematography

Marketing and Public Relations

Important skills: good listening skills, problem solving, public speaking, creativity

Important knowledge: writing, editing, technology, communications

College majors: marketing, public relations, journalism

GLOSSARY

blog (blawg): a webpage or website to which new messages are added easily

consultants (kuhn-SUHL-tuhnts): experts in a particular field who are hired by others to give advice

crucial (KROO-shuhl): decisive, extremely important for the success of something

encompass (en-KUHM-puhs): to include something

invention (in-VEN-chuhn): some useful thing that is newly designed or created

niche (nich): a place, job, or situation that suits someone very well

occupations (ahk-yuh-PAY-shuhnz): jobs or professions

personality (pur-suh-NAL-i-tee): all of the qualities and traits that make one person different from others

philosophy (fuh-LAH-suh-fee): the study of truth, wisdom, the nature of reality, and knowledge

revolution (rev-uh-LOO-shuhn): a sudden, radical, or far-reaching change

INDEX

data analysts 32, 33, 36

digital designers 29, 30

digital strategist(s) 20

Facebook 4, 5, 6, 8, 11, 14, 16, 18, 28, 29, 40

journalism 5

logo(s) 29, 31

marketing managers 36

printing press 11

public relations 26, 28, 39

social media manager(s) 16, 18, 36

software engineer(s) 13, 14, 15

startups 40

Twitter 4, 6, 16, 19, 20, 24, 28, 40

video producer(s) 34, 35

writers and editors 26, 27

SHOW WHAT YOU KNOW

1. What does a software engineer do?
2. What does a social media data analyst look for?
3. Who invented the printing press?
4. What was Android's original purpose?
5. How do most young people get their news today?

WEBSITES TO VISIT

www.commonsensemedia.org/lists/safe-chat-rooms-and-social-sites-for-kids#

http://engineeringforkids.com/programs

www.brainpop.com/technology

ABOUT THE AUTHOR

Kevin Walker is a father, writer, and editor who lives in Houston, Texas. He uses social media every day to do his job, keeping in touch with people all around the world. He also uses social media to share what's happening with friends, even if it's just something silly. *Especially* if it's just something silly.

Meet The Author!
www.meetREMauthors.com

www.rourkeeducationalmedia.com

PHOTO CREDITS: Cover: background © hybridtechno, phone © Happy Zoe, icons © rvlsoft; pages 4-5 logos © solomon7, youtube on iPad © Kaspars Grinvalds, youtube videos sreen © Lenscap Photography; page 6-7 guy © Anatoliy Karlyuk, girl © Syda Productions, phone wth Reddit © Zull Must, globe icon © Artistdesign13; page 8-9 iPhone © Krystof Sasek, icons © tanuha2001, kindle © Aleksandravicius; page 10-11 woman © zenstock, iPad © AlesiaKan, instagram on phone © Sattalat phukkum; page 12 phones © DeziDezi, tower © LOVELUCK; page13 © Ellica; page 14-15 Facebook screen shot © Pe3k, iPad © AlesiaKan, screenshot close-up © tuthelens; p16-17 © Rawpixel.com, iPhone © Kashin; p18-19 marketing plan © Rawpixel.com; page 20-21 © George Rudy; page 22 © fototrips, page 23 © Sergei Domashenko; page 24 © Fedorovekb, page 24-25 © Christian Bertrand; page 26-27 meeting © El Nariz, guy at computer © NakoPhotography ; page 28-29 © Rawpixel.com; page 30 nike swoosh © wonderpo99, page 31 REDPIXEL.PL; page 32 © PR Image Factory, page 33 © Rawpixel.com; page 34-35 crew © Lia Koltyrina, woman © PHILIPIMAGE, page 35 © Daniel Krason; page 36-37 © Rawpixel.com; page 38 expo © Kobby Dagan, page 39 tablet © Kuprevich; page 40 Mark Zuckerberg © catwalker; page 41 tablet © By Castlesk; page 42-43 © Jozsef Bagota, photo montage © twobee

All images Shutterstock.com except Superhero Central shot, Jack Dorsey photo © cellanr https://creativecommons.org/licenses/by-sa/2.0/deed.en ; Ben Silbermann photo © Anya https://creativecommons.org/licenses/by/2.0/deed.en ; Catarina Fake photo © Robert Scoble https://creativecommons.org/licenses/by/2.0/deed.en ;

Edited by: Keli Sipperley

Cover and Interior design by: Nicola Stratford   www.nicolastratford.com

Library of Congress PCN Data

STEAM Jobs in Social Media / Kevin Walker
(STEAM Jobs You'll Love)
ISBN 978-1-68342-394-2 (hard cover)
ISBN 978-1-68342-464-2 (soft cover)
ISBN 978-1-68342-560-1 (e-Book)
Library of Congress Control Number: 2017931285
Printed in the United States of America, North Mankato, Minnesota